G

You and Me

I Am Honest

Angela Leeper

Heinemann Library
Chicago, Illinois

© 2005 Heinemann Library,
a division of Reed Elsevier, Inc.
Chicago, Illinois

Customer Service 888-454-2279
Visit our website at www.heinemannlibrary.com

Designed by Mike Hogg (Maverick)
Printed and bound in China by South China Printing Company Limited
Photo research by Janet Lankford Moran

09 08 07 06 05
10 9 8 7 6 5 4 3 2 1

Library of Congress Cataloging-in-Publication Data
Leeper, Angela.
    I am honest / Angela Leeper.
        p. cm. -- (You and me)
    Includes index.
    ISBN 1-4034-6072-8 (hardcover) ISBN 1-4034-6080-9 (pbk.)
1. Honesty--Miscellanea--Juvenile literature. I. Title. II. Series.
    BJ1533.H7L44 2004
    179'.9--dc22
                            2004016609

3 1969 01636 3623

Acknowledgments
The author and publisher are grateful to the following for permission to reproduce copyright material:
Cover photograph by Janet Moran/Heinemann Library
pp. 4, 5 Que-Net/Heinemann Library; p. 6 Robert Lifson/Heinemann Library; pp. 7, 12, 13, 14, 15, 16, 17, 20, 21, 22, 23 Janet Moran/Heinemann Library; pp. 8, 9 Warling Studios/Heinemann Library; p. 10 Michael Newman/Photo Edit, Inc.; p. 11 Tom Prettyman/Photo Edit, Inc.; p. 18 Annie Griffiths Belt/Corbis; p. 19 Gabe Palmer/Corbis; back cover (L-R) Que-Net/Heinemann Library, Warling Studios/Heinemann Library

Every effort has been made to contact copyright holders of any material reproduced in this book.
Any omissions will be rectified in subsequent printings if notice is given to the publisher.

Many thanks to the teachers, library media specialists, reading instructors, and educational consultants who have helped develop the Read and Learn brand.

Contents

What Is Being Honest?

Being honest means telling the truth.

When you are honest you do not tell lies.

Being honest means telling a fact.

You do not say something that is made up.

Where Can You Be Honest?

You can be honest at home.

You can be honest at school, too.

You can be honest in your neighborhood.

Wherever you are, you can be honest.

Why Are You Honest?

People trust you when you are honest.

They believe what you say.

You are honest because it is the right thing to do.

Who Can You Be Honest With?

You can be honest with your parents.

You can be honest with your friends, too.

You can be honest with
your classmates.

You can be honest with everyone.

What Does It Look Like When You Are Honest?

When you are honest, other people may smile.

People are glad when you tell the truth.

People may help.

They may help you clean up
your mess.

What Does It Sound Like When You Are Honest?

You can say, "I did it."

You also can say, "I'm sorry."

When you are honest you may
hear someone say, "Thank you."

How Can You Be Honest at Home?

Your parents need your help at home.

When you are honest you do what they ask.

You do not say you are finished when you are not.

How Can You Be Honest at School?

You can tell the truth about your classmates.

Telling lies is not being honest.

You can do your own work.

Copying a classmate's work is not being honest.

How Do You Feel When You Are Honest?

You can feel proud when you are honest.

You can also feel happy.

Quiz

Who is being honest?

Answer to Quiz

This child is being honest.

She cleans up her mess.

Note to Parents and Teachers

Reading for information is an important part of a child's literacy development. Learning begins with a question about something. Help children think of themselves as investigators and researchers by encouraging their questions about the world around them. Each chapter in this book begins with a question. Read the question together. Look at the pictures. Talk about what you think the answer might be. Then read the text to find out if your predictions were correct. Think of other questions you could ask about the topic, and discuss where you might find the answers. Assist children in using the picture glossary and the index to practice new vocabulary and research skills.

Index